David Anders

OSINT: The Art of Collecting Open Information

Digital Society: The Growing Impact of Online Information Collection

Castle Editions

All rights reserved – August 2023

"Open intelligence is an invaluable source of information for security analysts and researchers. In an ever-changing digital world, OSINT has become an essential tool for understanding emerging threats, detecting vulnerabilities and anticipating potential risks."

John Doe, security and intelligence expert.

Summary

- FOREWORD 10
- **CHAPTER 1: INTRODUCTION TO OSINT** 14
  - DEFINITION OF OSINT AND ITS IMPORTANCE IN THE CURRENT CONTEXT. 14
  - HISTORY OF OSINT AND ITS APPLICATIONS IN THE PAST AND PRESENT. 17
    - *I. Beginnings of OSINT: From Antiquity to the Middle Ages* 18
    - *II. OSINT in the Modern Era: From Libraries to Print Media* 18
    - *III. The Digital OSINT Era: The Impact of the Internet* 19
    - *IV. Current applications of OSINT* 20
  - OSINT ETHICAL AND LEGAL PRINCIPLES. 21
    - *I. Transparency and Consent* 21
    - *II. Privacy* 22
    - *III. Relevance and Accuracy of Information* 22
    - *IV. Risk Minimization* 22
    - *V. Compliance with Laws and Regulations* 23
    - *VI. Responsible Use of Collected Information* 23
    - *VII. Protection of the Identity of Sources* 24
    - *VIII. Training and Awareness* 24
- **CHAPTER 2: OSINT METHODOLOGY** 25
  - THE DIFFERENT STAGES OF THE OSINT PROCESS: PLANNING, COLLECTION, ANALYSIS AND OPERATION. 25
    - *I. Planning* 26
    - *II. Data Collection* 27
    - *III. Analysis* 28
    - *IV. Operation* 29
  - MINDSET, ITERATION AND CONTINUOUS LEARNING 30
    - *I. The Mindset in OSINT* 30
    - *II. The importance of empirical iteration in OSINT* 31
    - *III. Monitoring OSINT techniques* 33
  - THE MANAGEMENT AND ORGANIZATION OF THE DATA COLLECTED. 34
    - *I. Structured collection* 34
    - *II. The relevant classification* 34
    - *III. Use of Metadata* 35
    - *IV. Secure Storage* 35
    - *V. Duplicate Management* 35
    - *VI. Data Updating* 36
    - *VII. Collaboration and Sharing* 36
    - *VIII. Ethical responsibility* 36

CHAPTER 3: OSINT TOOLS 38

- ADVANCED SEARCH ON SEARCH ENGINES 40
  - Specialized search engines 40
  - Advanced search on Google 43
  - OSINT Framework 45
- THE EXPLOITATION OF EMAIL 46
  - 1. EmailRep.io: 47
  - 2. Hunter.io: 47
  - 3. Have I Been Pwned: 48
  - 4. Dehashed: 48
  - 5. Maltiverse: 48
  - 6. MailTester.com: 49
  - 7. FullContact: 49
  - 8. Pipl: 49
  - 9. Spokeo: 50
  - 10. Social Searcher: 50
- DATA ANALYSIS 51
- BUSINESS RESEARCH 54
- PEOPLE RESEARCH 56
- THE EXPLOITATION OF NICKNAMES 58
- THE OPERATION OF WEBSITES 62
- THE EXPLOITATION OF TELEPHONE NUMBERS 67
- THE EXPLOITATION OF GEOLOCATION 70

CHAPTER 4: DATA ANALYSIS AND SORTING 74

- 1. OSINT DATA ANALYSIS TECHNIQUES TO EXTRACT RELEVANT INFORMATION 74
- 2. METHODS FOR VERIFYING THE SOURCES AND CREDIBILITY OF THE INFORMATION COLLECTED 76
- 3. USE OF DATA ANALYSIS TOOLS TO FACILITATE THE PROCESS 77

CHAPTER 5: OSINT AND THE FUTURE 79

- 1. PERSPECTIVES ON THE EVOLUTION OF OSINT IN THE COMING YEARS 79
- 2. NEW TRENDS AND EMERGING TECHNOLOGIES IN OSINT 80
- 3. POTENTIAL CHALLENGES FOR OSINT 82
- 4. ADAPT TO FUTURE CHANGES AND STAY AT THE FOREFRONT OF OSINT 83

CHAPTER 6: COUNTERMEASURES AND PERSONAL PROTECTION AGAINST OSINT 85

- OSINT PERSONAL PROTECTION POLICIES 85
- CONTROLLING ONLINE PRIVACY SETTINGS 85
- SOCIAL MEDIA MANAGEMENT 86
- USE OF PSEUDONYMS 86
- CAUTION WHEN ONLINE COMMUNICATION 86
- PASSWORD SECURITY 87
- MONITORING PERSONAL INFORMATION ONLINE 87

- Social Engineering Awareness 87
- Use of Information Deletion Tools 88
- Using a VPN 88
- OSINT Awareness 88
- Conclusion 88

CHAPTER 7: OSINT AND THE DARK WEB: EXPLORING THE HIDDEN DEPTHS OF THE INTERNET 90

- 1. Understanding the Dark Web 90
- 2. Access and Browsing the Dark Web 91
- 3. Dark Web Resources for OSINT 92
- 4. Analysis of Criminal Activities 92
- 5. Limitations and Challenges of Dark Web OSINT 93
- 6. OSINT Ethics on the Dark Web 93

CHAPTER 8: GOING FURTHER 95

- Francophone OSINT forums 95
- English-language OSINT forums 96
- English-language books on OSINT 96
- OSINT training 97
  - *IHEDN War School* 97
  - *EGE: School of Economic Warfare* 98
  - *Benefits of OSINT Training* 99

CONCLUSION: THE IMPACT OF OSINT ON OUR SOCIETY 101

Foreword

It's rare to encounter a field as dynamic and ever-evolving as online information gathering, also known as Open Source Intelligence (OSINT). In this book, we have the privilege of presenting you with a comprehensive guide on OSINT, authored by a renowned expert in the field: David Anderson.

David Anderson, a prominent figure in digital security and intelligence analysis, has established his expertise through an unrelenting passion for OSINT. Hailing from the United States, he has played a pivotal role in popularizing this method of online information collection, which has become a cornerstone in security, privacy protection, and countering emerging threats.

With a solid background in computer science and cybersecurity from Stanford University, David quickly distinguished himself as an independent researcher. He foresaw the increasing significance of OSINT in a world where digital data has become a goldmine of vital information. His exceptional career journey led him to found the Web Research Center, a renowned organization dedicated to analyzing digital trends and safeguarding online security.

At the heart of this book, you'll discover how David Anderson leveraged his experience and expertise to develop cutting-edge OSINT tools and advanced online information collection methods. His journey exemplifies how an ethical and responsible approach can make a significant contribution to the digital society by preserving privacy while enhancing security.

The work you hold in your hands is much more than a mere OSINT usage manual. It embodies a philosophy—a commitment from a specialist to illuminate the path towards responsible and productive use of this powerful approach. David Anderson shares his knowledge, expertise, and vision through these pages, providing an invaluable resource for security professionals, investigators, analysts, and all seeking to grasp the intricacies of OSINT.

Throughout the chapters, you'll be guided through fundamental OSINT concepts, collection and analysis methodologies, as well as advanced tools at your disposal. The book illustrates how OSINT has shaped the landscape of national security, justice, and cybersecurity, all while highlighting the importance of preserving privacy and ethics within this pursuit.

Through the history and biography of David Anderson, you'll encounter a person whose determination and expertise have propelled OSINT into the forefront of the digital security stage. It is with great enthusiasm that we invite you to delve into this book, to explore the limitless possibilities of OSINT, and to contribute to building a digital future that is safer, more transparent, and enlightened.

Let's not forget that online information gathering, when guided by skilled and ethical hands, can truly aid in preserving our ever-changing digital world.

Welcome to the fascinating realm of OSINT and the knowledge that David Anderson generously shares with us.

Chapter 1: Introduction to OSINT

OSINT (Open Source Intelligence) is an intelligence discipline that consists of collecting, analyzing and exploiting information from public sources and accessible to all. These sources include search engines, social networks, public databases, websites, online forums, media, government reports, and many others. Unlike traditional intelligence methods that are based on confidential sources, OSINT uses freely accessible information, without resorting to illegal or intrusive methods.

- **Definition of OSINT and its importance in the current context.**

OSINT occupies a prominent place in the current context due to the explosion of data available on the Internet and the increasing digitalization of society. The ease of access to online information and the proliferation of communication platforms have created an environment rich in open and publicly accessible data. This has ushered in a new era of opportunities and challenges, propelling OSINT to the forefront of intelligence gathering practices.

The importance of OSINT lies in its ability to provide fast and extensive access to a variety of information, making it invaluable for various applications. Whether in the field of security, criminal investigations, business, politics or geopolitics, OSINT offers considerable advantages for making informed decisions and anticipating threats.

In the field of security, OSINT plays a crucial role in detecting potential threats. Security researchers use OSINT to identify vulnerabilities, malware, ongoing attacks, and malicious actors. OSINT analysis can help anticipate attacks before they occur, identify sources of cyber threats, and understand the tactics, techniques, and procedures (TTPs) used by cybercriminals.

In the context of criminal investigations, OSINT has become an essential tool. Law enforcement agencies use OSINT to gather evidence, identify suspects, follow leads, locate missing persons and solve cases. OSINT provides crucial information to support investigations and contribute to the fight against crime.

In the business world, OSINT is widely used for competitive intelligence. Companies can monitor the activities of their competitors, track market trends, identify business opportunities and assess potential risks. OSINT analysis enables companies to make informed strategic decisions and remain competitive in an ever-changing business environment.

In the field of politics and geopolitics, OSINT is used by governments and political actors to gather information on other states, terrorist groups and other international actors. OSINT provides a better understanding of the intentions and actions of potential adversaries, predicts potential crises, and evaluates international relations.

However, the use of OSINT raises important ethical and legal questions. OSINT's ethical principles are based on respect for the individual rights, privacy and confidentiality of the persons concerned by the information collected. It is essential to collect and use data ethically, avoiding undue intrusion into the private sphere and complying with applicable data protection and privacy laws.

In addition, it is important to verify and validate information sources to avoid the spread of false information or misinformation. The accuracy and credibility of the information collected are fundamental elements of OSINT, and due diligence must be exercised in the collection and analysis process.

In short, OSINT has become an essential intelligence discipline in the current context. It provides unprecedented access to a vast amount of open information, which can be exploited in many areas. Whether for security, criminal investigations, business, politics or geopolitics, OSINT plays a key role in informed decision-making and understanding the world around us. However, it is essential to use OSINT ethically and responsibly, respecting the privacy of individuals and complying with applicable laws.

- **History of OSINT and its applications in the past and present.**

The history of OSINT dates back to ancient times, when the collection of open information already played an essential role in strategic and military decision-making. However, with the advent of the Internet and the explosion of data available online, OSINT has undergone a major evolution and has become a must-have intelligence discipline in the contemporary world. This chapter explores the history of OSINT, its past applications and its importance in the current context.

- *I. Beginnings of OSINT: From Antiquity to the Middle Ages*

The origins of OSINT date back to ancient times, when leaders and governments already used open information-gathering methods to monitor their enemies and assess military and political situations. Emissaries were sent to neighbouring territories to gather information on the intentions and movements of adversaries. Information obtained from open sources, such as traders, travelers, scholars and diplomats, was essential for making informed decisions.

In the Middle Ages, information gathering continued to play a key role in military and political strategies.

Spies were used to infiltrate enemy camps and gather intelligence on the plans and movements of opposing armies. The intercepted letters and documents also provided crucial information about leaders' intentions and political alliances.

- *II. OSINT in the Modern Era: From Libraries to Print Media*

With the advent of the printing press at the end of the fifteenth century, access to information became democratized, opening up new opportunities for the collection of open information. Libraries and universities have become important centres of knowledge, providing access to printed materials, maps, treaties and government reports.

In the nineteenth century, print media, such as newspapers and magazines, played a crucial role in the dissemination of information. Governments and intelligence agencies used these sources to monitor the activities of other countries and assess global political and economic trends. However, the collection of information at that time was mostly manual and required considerable effort to gather information from different sources.

- *III. The Digital OSINT Era: The Impact of the Internet*

The real OSINT revolution took place with the advent of the Internet at the end of the twentieth century. The development of search engines, such as Google, has transformed the way we access information. Now, a simple click could get a wealth of information on any subject. Social networks have also been instrumental in providing a platform to share personal information and opinions, creating a new source of open information.

In the 1990s, OSINT became a discipline in itself, with government agencies and companies creating units specifically dedicated to the collection and analysis of open information. Automated information collection has become possible through the development of data collection and analysis tools. Specialized search engines have been created to find specific information, such as Shodan, which allows searching for internet-connected devices.

- o *IV. Current applications of OSINT*

Today, OSINT is widely used in many areas, contributing significantly to security, criminal investigation, competitive intelligence and political decision-making activities. In the field of security, OSINT plays a crucial role in the early detection of threats. Security researchers use OSINT to identify vulnerabilities, malware, ongoing attacks, and malicious actors. OSINT analysis helps anticipate attacks and understand cybercriminals' TTPs.

In the context of criminal investigations, OSINT has become an essential tool for gathering evidence, identifying suspects, locating missing persons and solving cases. Law enforcement agencies use OSINT to follow leads and support investigations.

In the field of business, OSINT is widely used for competitive intelligence. Companies use OSINT to monitor the activities of their competitors, track market trends, and identify new business opportunities.

In the field of politics and geopolitics, OSINT is used by governments and political actors to gather information on other states and predict potential crises. OSINT's analysis provides a better understanding of the intentions and actions of global political actors.

- **OSINT Ethical and Legal Principles.**

We will review the ethical and legal principles of open information collection and highlight the importance of respecting individual rights, privacy and applicable laws.

- o *I. Transparency and Consent*

One of the fundamental ethical principles of open information gathering is transparency. It is essential to clearly inform the individuals concerned that their information is publicly available and may be collected and used for specific purposes. This is especially true for personal information, such as data on social media, online profiles, and public posts. Individuals must be aware of how their information is collected and used, and they must be given the opportunity to give informed consent.

- *II. Privacy*

The collection of open information must respect the privacy of individuals. Researchers and analysts should refrain from gathering information that is not directly relevant to the subject matter of their research or investigation. They should also avoid collecting sensitive or confidential information without proper authorization. Unauthorized disclosure of private data can invade the privacy of individuals and compromise their security.

- *III. Relevance and Accuracy of Information*

Information gathering should focus on relevant and reliable data. Researchers and analysts must ensure that they use credible sources and verify the accuracy of the information collected. The spread of false information or disinformation can have serious consequences and distort the conclusions drawn from the data.

- *IV. Risk Minimization*

When collecting open information, it is important to minimize the risks to the individuals whose information is collected. This means that researchers and analysts should avoid endangering the safety or well-being of the people concerned by the information collected. For example, when collecting information online, it is essential not to accidentally reveal information that could unintentionally identify or locate individuals.

- *V. Compliance with Laws and Regulations*

The collection of open information must comply with the laws and regulations in force in the country where it is carried out. Researchers and analysts should be aware of and comply with data protection, privacy, and information collection laws. This also includes respecting copyrights and licenses for the use of public data and online content.

- *VI. Responsible Use of Collected Information*

Information collected as part of the collection of open information must be used responsibly and ethically. Researchers and analysts must be careful not to use data for malicious purposes or to harm others. Misuse or inappropriate use of information may result in legal and ethical consequences.

- *VII. Protection of the Identity of Sources*

In some cases, the collection of open information may involve confidential sources who wish to remain anonymous. In such cases, it is essential to protect the identity of these sources and not to reveal their role in the collection of information. The protection of the identity of sources is essential to ensure their security and future cooperation.

- *VIII. Training and Awareness*

Researchers and analysts who collect open information must be trained and sensitized to the ethical and legal principles of this practice. A thorough knowledge of laws and regulations, as well as an understanding of the ethical issues related to the collection of information, are essential for the responsible use of OSINT.

Chapter 2: OSINT Methodology

OSINT is a complex process that requires a methodical and rigorous approach to achieving quality results. Unlike traditional intelligence methods that rely on confidential sources, OSINT relies on publicly available open information. This means that researchers must navigate an ocean of online data to extract relevant information while respecting ethical and legal principles.

OSINT's methodology includes several key steps, ranging from planning and research to analysis and presentation of results. Researchers need to be equipped with the right tools and techniques to collect and use data effectively. They should also be aware of the potential risks and ethical issues associated with collecting open information.

- **The different stages of the OSINT process: Planning, Collection, Analysis and Operation.**

The OSINT process involves several key steps, from initial planning to data collection, in-depth analysis and exploitation of the results obtained. Each step is essential to ensure effective, relevant and ethical information gathering.

  - *I. Planning*

Planning is the fundamental first step in the OSINT process. Before beginning to gather information, researchers should establish a clear and detailed plan to guide their approach. This step defines the specific objectives of the OSINT, identifies relevant sources of information and determines the tools and techniques to be used.

Define objectives: Researchers need to understand the specific needs of their OSINT project. They need to determine the questions they want to answer and the information they are looking for. This makes it possible to target the collection and ensure that the results obtained are relevant to the objectives set.

Identify sources of information: Once the objectives have been defined, researchers must identify the sources of information relevant to their project. These sources may include search engines, social networks, public databases, websites, online forums, media, and government reports, among others.

Determine tools and techniques: Based on the objectives and sources of information identified, researchers should select appropriate tools and techniques for information gathering. These tools may include advanced search engines, data aggregators, automated collection tools, data analysis tools, and visualization tools.

Assess risks and constraints: Before starting information gathering, researchers should assess the potential risks and constraints associated with their OSINT project. This may include issues related to privacy, security of confidential sources, and compliance with applicable laws and regulations.

- o *II. Data Collection*

Data collection is the central step in the OSINT process. Researchers should use the sources of information identified during planning to collect relevant and useful data.

Use specialized tools: Researchers should use specialized tools to collect information from identified sources of information. These tools can include advanced search engines, web crawlers, data aggregators, and automated collection tools.

Filter and sort data: With an abundance of information available online, researchers must be able to filter and sort data to collect only those that are relevant to their OSINT project. This step helps reduce noise and focus on important information.

Verify the accuracy of the data: During collection, it is essential to verify the accuracy of the data collected. Researchers should ensure that the information obtained is reliable and credible by verifying sources and cross-referencing information with other sources where possible.

- *III. Analysis*

Once the data is collected, researchers begin the analysis stage, which involves looking at information from different angles, looking for links and patterns, and drawing relevant conclusions.

Organize data: Before conducting analysis, researchers should organize the collected data in a way that makes it easier to extract useful information. This may include structuring data, categorizing information, and creating databases.

Search for links and patterns: OSINT analysis often involves looking for links and patterns between different information collected. This allows for deeper conclusions and an understanding of the relationships between actors and events.

Use advanced analysis techniques: Depending on the complexity of the OSINT project, researchers may use advanced analysis techniques, such as social network analysis, data mining, and text analysis.

- *IV. Operation*

The final step in the OSINT process is the exploitation of the results obtained. Researchers should interpret the conclusions of the analysis and relate them to the original objectives of the OSINT.

Interpret results: Researchers must interpret the results of the analysis objectively and impartially. They should identify key information and key conclusions drawn from the data collected.

Recommendations and actions: Based on the results of the analysis, researchers can formulate recommendations and actions to be taken. These recommendations can be used to make informed decisions in a security, investigation, business, or policy context.

Report and Presentation: Finally, researchers are expected to present OSINT results in the form of reports or presentations. The report should be clear, concise and accessible to relevant stakeholders.

- **Mindset, iteration and continuous learning**

To succeed in this practice, it is essential to have the right mindset and understand the importance of empirical iteration in the OSINT process. This approach helps to develop a better understanding of the information collected, minimize errors, and obtain more accurate and relevant results.

   o *I. The Mindset in OSINT*

The OSINT mindset is a set of attitudes and mental skills that promote effective and ethical information gathering. OSINT professionals must develop a mindset that fosters curiosity, perseverance, questioning and open-mindedness.

Curiosity: OSINT researchers need to be curious and knowledge-hungry. They should ask questions, actively seek information, and explore different sources to get a holistic view of the topic being studied.

Perseverance: Gathering open information can be complex and demanding. Researchers must be persistent in overcoming obstacles and continuing their efforts even in the face of fragmentary or hard-to-obtain data.

Critical thinking: Critical thinking is essential in OSINT. Researchers must be able to assess the credibility of sources, verify the accuracy of information, and identify possible biases.

Open-mindedness: OSINT researchers must be open to new ideas and approaches. They must be prepared to question their assumptions and consider different points of view to get a more complete view of the subject being studied.

- *II. The importance of empirical iteration in OSINT*

Empirical iteration, also known as the "learning loop," is an iterative process in which researchers collect information, analyze it, draw conclusions, and then adjust their approach based on the results obtained. This cyclical approach makes it possible to gradually improve the quality and relevance of the information collected.

Continuous learning: Empirical iteration promotes continuous learning. By repeating the collection and analysis process, researchers can identify errors and gaps in their methods, and thus improve their approach as the process progresses.
Training and skills development: OSINT researchers are expected to participate in trainings, workshops and seminars to enhance their technical skills and understanding of OSINT core principles.

Monitoring technological advances: OSINT is closely linked to technological developments. Researchers need to keep abreast of new technologies, software tools, and innovations that can improve their efficiency and accuracy in gathering information.

Knowledge sharing: The OSINT community is dynamic and collaborative. Researchers need to share their knowledge and experiences with their peers to enrich OSINT's overall knowledge base.

Method optimization: Empirical iteration optimizes information gathering methods. By adjusting and adapting their approach based on the results obtained, researchers can maximize the effectiveness of their approach.

Error minimization: By repeating the collection and analysis process, researchers can minimize errors and potential biases. They can check the results obtained repeatedly to ensure their reliability and accuracy.

In-depth understanding: Empirical iteration allows for the development of a thorough understanding of the subject being studied. By looking at the information collected from different angles and comparing it to different sources, researchers can get a more complete and nuanced view of the topic.

- o *III. Monitoring OSINT techniques*

Monitoring OSINT techniques is crucial to stay at the forefront of information gathering methods and good practices in the field. This allows researchers to benefit from the latest advances and the best methods to carry out their work more efficiently.

OSINT Community Monitoring: Researchers should follow OSINT blogs, forums, discussion groups and social networks to keep abreast of the latest trends, new techniques and emerging tools.

Reading articles and publications: OSINT researchers should read specialized articles and publications on the subject to keep abreast of new methods of information gathering and recommended good practices.

Participation in conferences and webinars: Researchers can participate in OSINT conferences and webinars to hear from experts in the field, share knowledge and expand their professional network.

- **The management and organization of the data collected.**

In the mysteries of open intelligence, the effective management of collected data is the key that opens the door to understanding. Once researchers have gone through the maze of information and extracted the precious nuggets, the crucial question arises: how to concretely manage these treasures of information to extract maximum value?

- o *I. Structured collection*

Collecting open information often starts with the use of specific search techniques and dedicated tools. Researchers should be organized from the outset, carefully noting the sources consulted, the keywords used, the websites visited, and the information obtained. A simple spreadsheet can be a powerful tool to capture these essential details, enabling structured data collection.

- o *II. The relevant classification*

Once the data is collected, the classification task comes into play. Researchers can create categories that reflect the objectives of their OSINT project. For example, if the project is about a survey of an organization, the categories could be "personnel", "finances", "partners", etc. Classification is a key step in organizing data in a logical and accessible way.

- o *III. Use of Metadata*

Metadata plays a crucial role in the management of the data collected. By adding additional information to the data, researchers can facilitate search, retrieval, and subsequent analysis. Metadata could include information about the source of the information, the date of collection, the reliability of the source, etc. These details will help researchers keep track of the information collected and assess its relevance.

- o *IV. Secure Storage*

Data security is a major concern when it comes to collecting open information. Researchers must ensure that the data collected is stored securely to prevent unauthorized access or accidental alteration. Encrypted and secure storage solutions should be considered to protect the integrity of the information collected.

- o *V. Duplicate Management*

Managing duplicates is an important step to avoid redundancies and potential errors in the collected data. Researchers should check the information collected to ensure that it has not been recorded multiple times. Data management tools can be used to identify and eliminate duplicates.

- *VI. Data Updating*

Data refresh is a key aspect of managing the information collected. In the OSINT field, information can change rapidly. It is therefore essential to keep the data up-to-date continuously, by regularly reviewing the sources and updating outdated information.

- *VII. Collaboration and Sharing*

In an open intelligence environment, collaboration is valuable. Researchers can work in teams to share the information collected, discuss results and exchange ideas. Online collaboration platforms can be used to facilitate data sharing and access among team members.

- *VIII. Ethical responsibility*

Finally, the management of the data collected must always be carried out in compliance with ethical and legal principles. Researchers should be aware of applicable laws and regulations regarding the collection, storage and use of personal data and sensitive information. Protecting the privacy of the individuals concerned must be a top priority.

In short, the concrete management of data collected in open intelligence requires a methodical and organized approach. Simple tools such as spreadsheets, well-defined categories, and detailed metadata can greatly facilitate information management. However, ethical responsibility remains at the heart of this discipline, as informed data management goes hand in hand with respect for privacy and individual rights. By combining curiosity, organization and ethics, OSINT researchers can fully exploit the data collected and make sense of the information, thus contributing significantly to intelligence, investigation and decision-making activities.

Chapter 3: OSINT Tools

In the ever-changing world of open intelligence, the power of information is unequivocal. For researchers engaged in the quest for hidden knowledge, OSINT tools prove to be indispensable companions. Although OSINT is an ever-changing discipline, this arsenal of tools provides a solid foundation for beginners eager to embark on the exciting adventure of collecting open information.

It is essential to note that the following list is not exhaustive, and covers only a fraction of the resources available in the OSINT universe. This discipline, in constant evolution, feeds on the creativity and insight of its practitioners. Every day, new tools and techniques emerge, transforming the OSINT landscape and offering unprecedented opportunities for those who know how to seize them.

For intelligence operators engaged in this quest for information, continuous learning is a pressing necessity. Practices that are cornerstones of OSINT today can be replaced by new, more innovative approaches tomorrow. A good OSINT researcher must stay abreast of the latest trends, keep up to date and constantly develop their knowledge and tool. This intellectual agility is a key skill that enables researchers to adapt to the changing challenges of the digital world.

In addition, intelligence operators must be vigilant in terms of confidentiality and ethics. The collection of open information must always comply with applicable laws and regulations, paying particular attention to the protection of the privacy of the individuals concerned. Responsible use of OSINT tools is the cornerstone of ethical and responsible practice.

In this chapter, we will explore a selection of basic tools that serve as a springboard for beginners into the captivating world of OSINT. Each tool offers unique perspectives for collecting and analyzing publicly available information. However, it is important to keep in mind that this list is only a starting point, and that exploring the multiple resources available in the OSINT field is a never-ending quest.

In summary, OSINT tools are indispensable companions to researchers probing the depths of public information. While embracing the wealth of resources at their disposal, intelligence operators must cultivate an unquenchable thirst for learning and development, as OSINT is an ever-evolving discipline. By combining prudence, ethics and perseverance, researchers can embark on this thrilling adventure, discovering the secrets hidden in the meanders of the digital world.

- **Advanced search on search engines**
    - *Specialized search engines*

Maltego:
Website: https://www.maltego.com/

Maltego is a powerful OSINT search engine that focuses on real-time data visualization. This ingenious tool collects and cross-checks information from various sources such as social networks, public databases, websites, etc. Maltego generates interactive graphs that allow researchers to better understand the connections between the different elements. Available in limited free version and more advanced paid versions, Maltego offers a user-friendly interface and state-of-the-art features for OSINT investigations.

Shodan:
Website: https://www.shodan.io/

Shodan is often referred to as a "search engine for connected objects". Unlike traditional search engines that index websites, Shodan crawls internet-connected objects such as surveillance cameras, servers, routers, etc. This allows researchers to discover devices that are potentially vulnerable to attacks or intrusions. Shodan offers paid subscriptions for advanced features, but also offers limited access for free.

Recon-ng:
Website: https://github.com/lanmaster53/recon-ng

Recon-ng is an open-source OSINT tool specifically designed for security and intelligence professionals. It allows advanced searches on social networks, search engines, messaging services, etc. Recon-ng automates the information gathering process using preconfigured modules, providing a methodical and structured approach to OSINT. This tool is free and constantly updated by the security research community.

FOCA (Fingerprinting Organizations with Collected Archives):
Website: https://github.com/ElevenPaths/FOCA

FOCA is an OSINT search engine specialized in identifying and analyzing metadata and hidden information in online files and documents. It is often used to collect information about organizations and their technical infrastructure. FOCA is available in two versions, one free and one more advanced paid.

Censys:
Website: https://censys.io/

Censys is an OSINT search engine dedicated to crawling digital certificates, servers, protocols, services, etc. It offers advanced features for vulnerability discovery and internet security monitoring. Censys offers paid subscriptions for more extensive searches, but it also offers a free version with limitations.

TheHarvester:
Website: https://github.com/laramies/theHarvester

TheHarvester is an open-source tool in Python, specialized in collecting targeted information in OSINT. It allows researchers to explore a variety of online sources to extract relevant data about domains, email addresses, usernames, subdomains, phone numbers, and more. TheHarvester performs queries on search engines, social networks, websites, public databases and presents the results in an organized way for later analysis.

- *Advanced search on Google*

Google, the undisputed search engine giant, is a must-have tool for many online tasks. While many users settle for basic searches, few know that Google offers powerful advanced features for open intelligence researchers. These features, often unknown, make it possible to refine searches and access more specific and targeted information. Here's a look at advanced Google search and how useful it is in the OSINT world.

Search Operators:

Search operators are special symbols or keywords that can be added to a Google query to filter results. For example, using "site:", one can limit the results to a specific website, or using "filetype:", one can search for specific files (for example, PDF files or Word documents). Search operators thus make it possible to refine the search and access more targeted information.

The quotation marks:

Using quotation marks around a search term (e.g., "artificial intelligence"), Google is told to search for exactly that phrase. This allows for more accurate results by excluding results that contain the words separately.

Exclusion of Terms:

By adding a minus sign ("-") in front of a search term (for example, "weather -Paris"), Google is told to exclude this term from the results. This is useful for filtering out results that are not relevant to the search.

Search in a Date Range:

Using Google's advanced search tools, it is possible to filter the results to match a specific date range. This makes it possible to focus on the most recent information or to find older elements for historical research.

File Search:

Using the "filetype:" operator, it is possible to search for specific files on the web. For example, "filetype:pdf artificial intelligence" will make it possible to find PDF documents related to artificial intelligence.

Search for Links:

The "link:" operator is used to find web pages that refer to a specific website. This can be useful for identifying sites that mention a specific organization or individual.

- OSINT Framework

OSINT Framework is a powerful and comprehensive tool designed to facilitate access to a multitude of OSINT resources from a centralized interface. It is an open-source web platform, which brings together hundreds of tools, links and sources of information useful to open intelligence researchers. OSINT Framework provides a comprehensive overview of available resources, optimizing and accelerating the information gathering process.

Website address: https://osintframework.com/

OSINT Framework comes in the form of a smart web that methodically organizes OSINT tools and sources into different categories. Researchers can easily navigate through the different sections to access tools and links relevant to their specific surveys. The platform also offers search listings for specific areas such as social networks, search engines, image analysis tools, public databases, etc.

The major advantage of OSINT Framework lies in its ability to centralize OSINT resources, which greatly facilitates the search for information. OSINT researchers can:

Quickly access a wide range of OSINT tools and sources from a single interface.
Optimize their workflow by using the specific search lists for each category of information. Benefit from frequent updates of the platform with new resources and tools.

- **The exploitation of Email**

Email, the ubiquitous element of modern digital communication, is an invaluable mine of information for open intelligence researchers. Leveraging email in OSINT (Open Source Intelligence) opens the doors to a world rich in hidden details, unsuspected connections and crucial evidence. Email addresses are often associated with a multitude of online entities, such as individuals, businesses, organizations, websites, and much more. By skillfully analyzing these electronic matches, researchers can decode networks, intentions, affiliations, and even vulnerabilities. However, the exploitation of e-mail in OSINT requires a methodical and privacy-friendly approach, in order to guarantee the ethics and legality of this quest for information.

In this section, we'll explore techniques and tools for leveraging email wisely in OSINT. From searching for email addresses, to analyzing headers and message content, to examining attachments and signatures, we'll dive into the intricacies of this demanding discipline. By understanding the nuances of leveraging email in OSINT, researchers will be able to enrich their investigations and uncover critical information hidden in the maze of digital correspondence.

- **1. EmailRep.io:**

Website: https://emailrep.io/

EmailRep.io is a powerful OSINT tool that allows you to gather in-depth information about an email address. It provides an assessment of the risk associated with the email, information about the sender's reputation, and details about the activity and associated links. The tool also scans email headers for possible phishing or spam attempts. EmailRep.io offers a simple and user-friendly interface for quick access to essential information about a specific email address.

- **2. Hunter.io:**

Website: https://hunter.io/

Hunter.io is an OSINT tool that specializes in finding business email addresses. It allows you to find email addresses associated with a specific domain, which is especially useful for finding business contacts.

Hunter.io also provides additional information such as the name of the contact, the position held, as well as information about the company.

- **3. Have I Been Pwned:**

Website: https://haveibeenpwned.com/

Have I Been Pwned is an OSINT service that allows you to check if an email address has been compromised during data breaches. It alerts the user if the email address is associated with data leaks or security breaches, which is essential to protect the privacy and security of online accounts.

- **4. Dehashed:**

Website: https://dehashed.com/

Dehashed is an email search engine that allows you to search for specific email addresses in stolen and publicly disclosed databases. It provides detailed results that can include passwords, highlighting the security risks of using a specific email.

- **5. Maltiverse:**

Website: https://www.maltiverse.com/

Maltiverse is an OSINT tool that allows you to search for information about a specific email address in a multitude of intelligence sources, including phishing lists, malicious sites, and potential threats. It offers a complete view of the presence of the email address in the digital ecosystem.

- **6. MailTester.com:**

Website: https://mailtester.com/

MailTester.com is a simple but effective OSINT tool that allows you to check if an email address is valid and functional. It sends a test email to check if the email address is real and active, which is useful to avoid sending emails to non-existent addresses.

- **7. FullContact:**

Website: https://www.fullcontact.com/

FullContact is an OSINT tool that allows you to enrich the information associated with an email address. It provides details about the owner of the address, such as social media profiles, phone numbers, postal addresses, etc. This provides a more complete view of the contact associated with the email.

- **8. Pipl:**

Website: https://pipl.com/

Pipl is an OSINT search engine that allows you to find information about a person from their email address. It crawls public databases, social networks, websites, archives, and other sources to provide details about the email owner, such as online profiles, affiliations, and more.

- **9. Spokeo:**

Website: https://www.spokeo.com/

Spokeo is an OSINT tool that allows you to search for information about a person from their email address. It provides details about social media profiles, postal addresses, phone numbers, and other public information related to the email address being searched.

- o **10. Social Searcher:**

Website: https://www.social-searcher.com/

Social Searcher is an OSINT tool that allows you to search for a specific email address on social networks. It allows you to discover the profiles associated with the email on the different social platforms, thus allowing to better understand the identity and interactions of the owner of the email address.

These tools offer varied perspectives for leveraging an OSINT email address, providing additional information for in-depth surveys and analysis. However, it is essential to use them responsibly and ethically, respecting the privacy of the individuals concerned and complying with applicable laws and regulations.

- **Data analysis**

OSINT data analysis is a crucial step in extracting meaningful insights from a large volume of collected data. This intelligent exploration is facilitated by a range of specialized tools that allow data to be processed, organized, and visualized more efficiently. Here is a selection of powerful tools for OSINT data analysis:

SpiderFoot:
Website: https://www.spiderfoot.net/

SpiderFoot is an open-source data analysis tool that automates the process of gathering information in OSINT. It gathers data from different sources such as search engines, social networks, public databases, DNS services, and many others. SpiderFoot then organizes this information by categorizing it into specific categories, allowing researchers to analyze it more efficiently.

Metagoofil :
Website: https://github.com/laramies/metagoofil

Metagoofil is a data analysis tool specifically designed to extract information from files (e.g. Word documents, PDFs) available on public websites. It searches for and collects metadata and hidden information in these files to provide valuable details about associated organizations or individuals.

Tineye:

Website: https://tineye.com/

Tineye is a reverse search engine for OSINT images. It allows searchers to search for a specific image on the web to find other versions, similar uses, or similar images. This can be useful for identifying the origin and dissemination of images, and even for tracing the online presence of individuals or organizations.

Gephi:
Website: https://gephi.org/

Gephi is a graph analysis tool that allows you to visualize and analyze relational data interactively. It is useful for exploring the links between entities and detecting hidden patterns in the data.

CARTO:
Website: https://carto.com/

CARTO is a geospatial data analysis platform in OSINT. It maps and visualizes geolocated data to better understand geographic trends and spatial relationships.

Grep:
Website: https://www.gnu.org/software/grep/

Grep is a command-line tool that allows you to search for specific patterns in text files. It is a simple yet powerful tool for filtering and extracting relevant information from large amounts of textual data.

IBM i2 Analyst's Notebook:
Website: https://www.ibm.com/uk-en/products/i2-analysts-notebook

IBM i2 Analyst's Notebook is a data analysis and link visualization tool used by security and intelligence professionals. It allows you to visually connect information to detect complex patterns and relationships between entities.

- **Business research**

Business research is a key area in OSINT, providing valuable information about companies, their activities, affiliations, and links with other entities. Here is a selection of four specialized tools that facilitate business research:

OCCRP Aleph:
Website: https://aleph.occrp.org/

OCCRP Aleph is a journalistic investigative database that brings together an extensive collection of documents and information on companies around the world. This OSINT tool provides access to data from leaked documents, investigative reports, and other public information sources. OCCRP Aleph is an invaluable resource for open intelligence researchers looking to dig deep into business operations.

Offshore Leaks Database:
Website: https://offshoreleaks.icij.org/

Offshore Leaks Database is a platform developed by the International Consortium of Investigative Journalists (ICIJ) that sheds light on the offshore financial activities of companies and individuals. The OSINT tool provides information on companies, directors, shareholders and links between offshore entities. It allows researchers to uncover information about international financial transactions and opaque structures used by certain companies.

OpenCorporates:
Website: https://opencorporates.com/

OpenCorporates is a corporate database that lists information on millions of companies around the world. This OSINT tool provides access to public data from official registries, governments and other reliable sources. OpenCorporates allows researchers to search for companies by name, identification number, or geographic location, and provides details about their legal status, history, and executives.

Company.ninja:
Website: https://societe.ninja/

Societe.ninja is an OSINT tool specialized in research on companies in France. It allows researchers to find information about French companies using their name or identification number. The tool provides details about the state of the company, its executives, its share capital, and other essential information.

These specialized tools offer a variety of information to explore the entrepreneurial universe and conduct in-depth surveys of companies. By combining these resources with data analysis techniques and a methodical approach, researchers can gain valuable insights for their investigations, case studies, and in-depth analyses of companies' economic and financial activities.

- **People Research**

OSINT research is a quest to uncover information about specific individuals, their online profiles, affiliations, and activities. Here is a selection of specialized tools that make it easier to find people:

Hunter.io:
Website: https://hunter.io/

Even if we have already presented it Hunter.io, it is a powerful and usable tool for research on people. It allows you to find email addresses associated with a specific domain, which is especially useful for searching for business contacts.

Lusha:
Website: https://www.lusha.com/

Lusha is an OSINT tool that allows you to find contact information about individuals from their name and company. It provides phone numbers and email addresses, making it easy to approach people in a professional context.

Pipl:
Website: https://pipl.com/

Pipl is an OSINT search engine that allows you to find information about a person based on their name, email address, phone number or username. It crawls public databases, social networks, websites, and other sources to provide details about who owns the ID you're looking for.

Social networks:

Social networks are an essential source of OSINT information about people. Popular platforms such as Facebook, LinkedIn, Twitter, Instagram and many others provide access to profiles, posts, logins and other personal information about individuals.

TruePeopleSearch:
Website: https://www.truepeoplesearch.com/

TruePeopleSearch is an OSINT search engine that allows you to find information about people from their name, address or phone number. It provides details such as address, phone number, background, and associated affiliations.

Creepy:
Website: https://github.com/ilektrojohn/creepy

Creepy is an OSINT tool that collects information about individuals from their social media activities. It gathers geolocation data, photos and other information available on users' social profiles.

- **The exploitation of nicknames**

The search and exploitation of pseudonyms are important aspects in OSINT, allowing to discover information about individuals who use different online identities. Here are some other OSINT tools that can be used to exploit pseudonyms:

Sherlock:
Website: https://github.com/sherlock-project/sherlock

Sherlock is an OSINT tool specialized in searching for user profiles through social networks. It allows you to search for a specific nickname on different platforms to find the profiles associated with that nickname.

Social-searcher:
Website: https://www.social-searcher.com/

Social-Searcher is an OSINT search engine dedicated to exploring social networks. It allows you to search for a specific pseudonym to find the associated profiles on the different social platforms.

Knowem:
Website: https://knowem.com/

Knowem is an OSINT tool that allows you to check the availability of a pseudonym on social networks and websites. It offers an advanced search function to find existing profiles related to this pseudonym.

Pipl:
Website: https://pipl.com/

Pipl, mentioned earlier for research on people, can also be used to explore pseudonyms. It allows searching for a specific nickname to find information and related online profiles.

Yandex:
Website: https://yandex.com/

Yandex is a Russian search engine that can be used to search for information about a pseudonym in Russian results. It offers a different perspective than other traditional search engines.

PeekYou:
Website: https://www.peekyou.com/

PeekYou is an OSINT search engine that allows you to search for information about people, including those using pseudonyms, based on their name, nickname, or username on social networks.

Namechk:
Website: https://namechk.com/

Namechk is an OSINT tool that allows you to check the availability of a pseudonym on social networks, websites and online platforms. It provides information about existing profiles linked to this pseudonym.

Tinfoleak:
Website: https://github.com/vaguileradiaz/tinfoleak

Tinfoleak is an OSINT tool that collects information about users and activities on Twitter. It can be used to exploit pseudonyms by searching for information associated with that pseudonym on Twitter.

Maigret:
Website: https://github.com/soxoj/maigret

Maigret is an OSINT tool specialized in searching for user profiles on social networks. It allows searching for a specific nickname on a variety of social platforms, including Twitter, Instagram, Reddit, and many others. Maigret provides direct links to found profiles, making it easier to explore the online identities associated with that pseudonym.

WhatsMyName:
Website: https://github.com/WebBreacher/WhatsMyName

WhatsMyName is an OSINT tool developed by WebBreacher that allows searching for a specific nickname on different online platforms, including social networks, websites, forums, and others. It provides detailed results for each platform, making it easier to identify profiles associated with the pseudonym you are looking for.

These tools offer a variety of approaches to explore the online identity of individuals using pseudonyms. By combining them with other tools and a methodical approach, researchers can uncover hidden information about people who operate under different identities online.

- **The operation of websites**

Searching and operating websites are key elements of OSINT, uncovering information about domains, servers, web pages and changes over time. Here are some specialized OSINT tools for crawling websites:

Domain Big Data:
Website: https://domainbigdata.com/

Domain Big Data is an OSINT platform that allows you to search for detailed information about a specific domain name. This tool provides details such as WHOIS records, associated IP addresses, mail servers, domain owners, and change of ownership histories.

Rapid DNS:
Website: https://rapiddns.io/

Rapid DNS is an OSINT tool that allows you to collect DNS records for a specific domain name. It provides information about DNS records, such as A, MX, NS, and TXT records, allowing researchers to better understand the technical infrastructure of the domain.

SpiderFoot:
Website: https://www.spiderfoot.net/

SpiderFoot, mentioned earlier for data analysis, can also be used for website operation. This OSINT tool gathers information from a variety of sources, including websites, social networks, search engines, and public databases, to provide a comprehensive view of a specific domain name.

Urlscan.io:
Website: https://urlscan.io/

Urlscan.io is an online service that allows you to scan and analyze web pages in real time. It captures a screenshot of the web page, extracts related resources, and provides information about destination domains, network requests, and executed scripts.

Wayback Machine:
Website: https://archive.org/web/

Wayback Machine is a web archiving service offered by the Internet Archive. It allows you to consult archived versions of websites at different points in time. This can be particularly useful for exploring changes and evolutions of a website over time.

Whois Lookup:
Website: https://who.is/

Whois Lookup is an online tool that allows you to search for WHOIS information about a specific domain name. It provides details about the domain owner, contact information, when the domain was created, and much more. This tool is commonly used to find the owner of a domain name.

DomainTools:
Website: https://www.domaintools.com/

DomainTools is an OSINT service specialized in domain name mining and searching. It offers detailed domain information, including WHOIS records, ownership histories, domain relationships, and associated contact information.

IPinfo:
Website: https://ipinfo.io/

IPinfo is an OSINT service that allows you to find information about a specific IP address, including the web host. It also provides details such as Internet Service Provider (ISP), geographic location, and geographic coordinates associated with the IP address.

Wappalyzer:
Website: https://www.wappalyzer.com/

Wappalyzer is a browser extension and online tool that can detect technologies used on a website. It can identify CMS, frameworks, programming languages, analysis tools, and many other elements of the site's code.

BuiltWith:
Website: https://builtwith.com/

BuiltWith is an OSINT tool that provides detailed information about the technologies used on a website. It offers details about servers, CMS, frameworks, JavaScript libraries, plugins, analytics tools and much more.

SecurityHeaders:
Website: https://securityheaders.com/

SecurityHeaders is an online tool for checking the HTTP security headers of a website. It indicates whether the site uses recommended security headers to protect against web attacks.

JSDetox:
Website: https://github.com/restran/jsdetox

JSDetox is a JavaScript obfuscation detection analysis tool. It helps reveal hidden parts of JavaScript code that could be used to mask malicious intent.

Burp Suite:
Website: https://portswigger.net/burp

Burp Suite is a suite of security scanning tools that includes a proxy to intercept and modify web traffic. It can be used to examine a website's traffic and source code in detail.

Chrome Developer Tools:
Website: https://developer.chrome.com/docs/devtools/

Chrome Developer Tools are built into the Google Chrome browser and allow you to inspect a website's source code, modify CSS and JavaScript in real time, and debug client-side code.

These tools offer a variety of approaches for exploring and analyzing OSINT websites. By combining these tools with other resources and a methodical approach, researchers can uncover hidden insights into domains, servers, web pages, and historical changes, for in-depth investigations into online actors and digital activities.

- **The exploitation of telephone numbers**

The search and exploitation of telephone numbers are important aspects of OSINT, allowing information to be discovered about the owners of the numbers, their affiliations and their online activities. Here are three specialized OSINT tools for exploiting phone numbers:

Epios Phone Number :
Website: https://epios.net/phone-number

Epios Phone Number is an OSINT tool that allows you to search for information about a specific phone number. It provides details such as carrier, geographic location, phone type, and other useful information about the number.

PhoneInfoga:
Website: https://github.com/sundowndev/PhoneInfoga

PhoneInfoga is an OSINT tool specialized in searching for information about phone numbers. It allows you to find information about the number, such as country, carrier, phone type, geographic location, associated online profiles, and much more.

TrueCaller:

Website: https://www.truecaller.com/

TrueCaller is an online service and mobile app that helps identify unknown phone numbers. It uses a global database of users who have chosen to share their information, which makes it possible to discover the name and profile associated with a phone number.

Numverify : Website: https://numverify.com/
Numverify is an OSINT tool for checking and finding information about international phone numbers. It provides details such as country, carrier, geographical location, and number status.

OSINT Combine: Website: https://osintcombine.com/
OSINT Combine is an OSINT platform that combines multiple data sources into a single report. It allows you to search for information about a phone number, email address, name, or company, and provides a comprehensive report of the results.

Phone Validator:
Website: https://phonevalidator.com/

Phone Validator is an online tool for validating phone numbers and obtaining information about their validity. It can be used to check if a phone number is active and used.

Spytox:
Website: https://www.spytox.com/

Spytox is an OSINT search engine that allows you to find information about phone numbers, email addresses, names, and profiles online. It gathers data from public sources to provide detailed results.

Hushed:
Website: https://hushed.com/

Hushed is a mobile application that allows you to generate temporary phone numbers for online privacy. This can be useful when creating online accounts or communicating with unknown people.

These tools offer various features for exploring OSINT phone numbers. By using them responsibly and ethically, researchers can uncover relevant information about number owners, their affiliations, and online activities, which can be useful for surveys, case studies, and in-depth analysis.

- **The exploitation of geolocation**

Geolocation is an essential aspect of OSINT, allowing you to discover information about the geographical location of people, devices or websites. Here are three specialized OSINT tools for the exploitation of geolocation:

Bing Maps and Google Maps:

Websites: https://www.bing.com/maps/ and https://www.google.com/maps/

Bing Maps and Google Maps are popular online mapping services that allow you to search for places, get driving directions, and display satellite and Street View views. These tools can be used to explore geographic locations associated with GPS coordinates, addresses, or other geotagged information.

GeoIP Lookup:
Website: https://www.geoiplookup.io/

GeoIP Lookup is an online tool that allows you to geolocate a specific IP address. It provides details such as country, region, city, geographic coordinates, and ISP associated with the IP address.

Wigle.net:
Website: https://wigle.net/

Wigle.net is an online database that allows you to search and visualize Wi-Fi networks around the world. It offers information about Wi-Fi access points, including the geographical addresses where these access points have been detected.

Geosetter:
Website: https://www.geosetter.de/

Geosetter is a geolocation software that allows you to geotag photos by assigning them GPS coordinates. It can also display location data on an interactive map.

MarineTraffic:
Website: https://www.marinetraffic.com/

MarineTraffic is a real-time tracking service for vessels worldwide. It allows you to geolocate ships, view their itinerary and view detailed information about each ship.

GPS Visualizer:
Website: https://www.gpsvisualizer.com/

GPS Visualizer is an online tool for converting and plotting GPS location data on an interactive map. It supports different GPS file formats.

IP Location:
Website: https://iplocation.com/

IP Location is an online service that allows you to geographically locate an IP address. It provides information about the country, region, city, and geographic coordinates associated with the IP address.

FlightRadar24:
Website: https://www.flightradar24.com/

FlightRadar24 is a real-time flight tracking service that can locate aircraft in the sky using their ADS-B transponders.

iTrack Wildlife:
Website: https://www.itrackwildlife.com/

iTrack Wildlife is a mobile application designed to track and record wildlife sightings in the field using geolocation.

Geocode Farm:
Website: https://www.geocodefarm.com/
Geocode Farm is an online service that allows you to geocode addresses and convert them into geographical coordinates (latitude and longitude).

These tools offer different approaches to explore and exploit geolocation in OSINT. By using these tools ethically and legally, researchers can discover relevant information about geographic locations associated with IP addresses, devices, Wi-Fi networks, and much more. Geolocation can be a key element in tracking online activity, locating individuals or organizations, and making informed decisions through in-depth investigations.

Chapter 4: Data Analysis and Sorting

Open Source Intelligence (OSINT) is full of diverse and abundant data from publicly available open sources. The effectiveness of OSINT lies in the ability to sort, analyse and extract relevant information from this mass of information. In this chapter, we will explore OSINT data analysis techniques to extract useful and reliable information. We will also discuss methods for verifying the sources and credibility of the information collected, as well as the use of data analysis tools to facilitate the process.

- **1. OSINT data analysis techniques to extract relevant information**

OSINT data analysis involves looking for patterns, connections, and gathering key information to get a clear picture of the situation. Here are some common OSINT data analysis techniques:

a) Linkage and connection analysis: One of the key techniques of OSINT analysis is to examine the links and connections between different entities. This can include analyzing relationships between people, organizations, websites, IP addresses, phone numbers, etc. Social network analysis tools, such as Gephi, can be used to visualize and analyze the links between entities.

b) Social Media Analytics: Social media is a valuable source of OSINT information. Analysis of posts, interactions, and social profiles can provide information about the activities, interests, affiliations, and relationships of individuals and organizations.

c) **Content analysis:** Content analysis is the process of examining text, images, and videos for key information. The use of keywords, specific phrases and contexts makes it possible to filter data and extract relevant information.

(d) **Geospatial analysis: Geospatial** analysis involves mapping geolocated data to identify patterns, clusters and geographic trends.

e) **Temporal analysis: Temporal** analysis tracks changes and changes in activities over time, which can be essential for understanding patterns of behaviour.

f) **Metadata analysis** : Metadata analysis, such as email header information or EXIF data from photos, can provide additional details about the origin and author of the data.

2. Methods for verifying the sources and credibility of the information collected

Verification of sources and credibility of information is essential in OSINT to ensure that the data collected is reliable and accurate. Here are some methods to verify sources and information:

a) Cross-reference sources: Check the information by cross-referencing it with other independent sources. If several reliable sources confirm a piece of information, it is more likely to be credible.

b) Assess the reputation of the source: Research the reputation of the source to determine its credibility. Well-established and reputable sources are generally more reliable.

c) Analyze the context: Examine the context in which the information was published. Be wary of information that is out of context or information that can be distorted.

d) Check information with official sources: If possible, check information directly with official or recognized sources to confirm its accuracy.

e) Identify potential biases: Be aware of potential biases that could affect information. Seek balanced and unbiased views.

- **3. Use of data analysis tools to facilitate the process**

Using OSINT data analysis tools can speed up and improve the exploration and analysis process. Here are some useful OSINT data analysis tools:

a) Maltego: Maltego is a network analysis tool that visualizes the links between entities and explores OSINT relationships.

b) SpiderFoot: SpiderFoot is an automated OSINT tool that performs a comprehensive target analysis by searching for information about domains, IP addresses, email addresses, usernames, etc.

c) FOCA: FOCA is a tool for collecting metadata from documents and files to extract information about an organization.

d) Google dorks: Google dorks are special search queries that filter search results to find specific information. They can be useful for OSINT exploration.

e) YARA: YARA is a malicious code detection tool that can be used to look for specific signatures in collected files and data.

f) Shodan: Shodan, mentioned earlier, can also be used to analyze research data and find vulnerable or misconfigured devices.

Using these data analysis techniques and source verification methods, as well as appropriate data analysis tools, OSINT researchers can refine and extract relevant, reliable and meaningful information from the vast volumes of data available in OSINT. Thorough and thoughtful analysis is key to turning raw data into actionable insights. However, it is important to keep in mind that OSINT analysis requires a balance between the use of tools and the exercise of human judgment to ensure the quality and integrity of the information collected.

Chapter 5: OSINT and the Future

Open Source Intelligence (OSINT) is an ever-evolving field, and in this chapter we will look at the prospects for its development in the coming years. We will also discuss new trends, emerging technologies and potential challenges that OSINT may face. Finally, we will discuss ways to adapt to the coming changes and stay at the forefront of OSINT.

- **1. Perspectives on the evolution of OSINT in the coming years**

OSINT already plays a crucial role in the areas of security, intelligence, investigations and decision-making. With the continued proliferation of online data and the rapid expansion of the cyber sphere, OSINT will become even more important in capturing the increasing complexity of the digital environment. As more people and organizations embrace digital as their primary means of communication and information sharing, OSINT will become an invaluable source of intelligence on online behavior, hidden agendas, suspicious activity and potential threats.

One of the major prospects for OSINT's evolution is its increasing integration with artificial intelligence (AI) and machine learning (ML) technologies. AI and ML have already brought significant advances in OSINT by automating some data collection and analysis tasks. For example, AI algorithms can be used to automatically monitor thousands of online information sources, detect patterns of suspicious activity, and identify significant trends. Predictive analytics, enabled by AI, could also be used to assess potential risks and anticipate future threats.

- **2. New trends and emerging technologies in OSINT**

AI and ML in OSINT: Artificial intelligence and machine learning have the potential to fundamentally transform the way OSINT is conducted. Machine learning algorithms can help sort, filter, and analyze large amounts of data online, allowing OSINT researchers to focus on the most relevant information. In addition, AI can be used to improve the detection of fake accounts and misleading information, thereby enhancing the reliability of sources.

Natural Language Processing (NLP): Natural language processing is another emerging technology that will have a significant impact on OSINT. NLP techniques allow computers to understand and analyze human language, which can be extremely useful for analyzing large amounts of online text, such as news articles, social media posts, and discussion forums. This will allow OSINT researchers to quickly detect trends and topics of interest, and identify public opinions and feelings on specific topics.

Internet of Things (IoT): With the increasing proliferation of internet-connected objects, such as security cameras, sensors and smart devices, OSINT will have access to more real-time data from physical sources. For example, traffic sensors, surveillance cameras and GPS devices could provide useful information for mapping the movement of people and goods. This could be particularly valuable for criminal investigations and security operations.

Advanced geospatial analysis: Geospatial OSINT is also expected to see significant advances. Advanced geolocation, mapping and satellite imagery technologies will enable a more detailed analysis of the physical environment. This could help identify areas of concentration of certain activities, track the movement of people or vehicles, and identify sensitive infrastructure. This information could be useful for criminal investigations, security operations and intelligence activities.

- **3. Potential challenges for OSINT**

With the rapid evolution of OSINT and the adoption of new technologies, new challenges will also emerge. Some of the potential challenges OSINT could face include:

Information overload: One of the main challenges for OSINT researchers is information overload. The amount of data available online is huge and constantly expanding. This makes it increasingly difficult to sort and filter relevant information. Researchers will need to exercise judgment in selecting sources and data for analysis.

Privacy: With the explosion of online data, the issue of privacy is becoming a growing concern. OSINT researchers will need to be mindful of the collection of sensitive data and ensure compliance with data protection laws and regulations. In addition, they will need to take steps to protect their own privacy and security when conducting online investigations.

Disinformation countermeasures: As OSINT is increasingly used for information gathering, hostile actors can put in place countermeasures to scramble sources of information and spread false information. OSINT researchers will therefore need to be vigilant in identifying unreliable sources and verifying the credibility of information collected from multiple independent sources.

Data security: With the increasing use of digital tools and cloud services for the collection and storage of OSINT data, data security will become a major challenge. OSINT researchers will need to implement robust security measures to protect their data from cyberattacks and privacy breaches.

- **4. Adapt to future changes and stay at the forefront of OSINT**

To stay at the forefront of OSINT and adapt to future changes, OSINT researchers must take a proactive and continuous learning approach. Here are some strategies to adapt to future changes:

Training and skills updating: OSINT researchers need to keep abreast of the latest trends and new technologies in OSINT. This can be achieved through trainings, online courses, conferences and seminars.

Collaboration and information sharing: Collaboration with other OSINT researchers and security agencies can be very beneficial. This allows for the sharing of knowledge, best practices and information on new threats and emerging trends.

Monitoring trends: OSINT researchers should closely monitor emerging trends in cybercrime, disinformation and new technologies. This will enable them to anticipate future challenges and develop appropriate adaptation strategies.

Compliance with regulations and ethics: OSINT researchers should be aware of data collection and privacy regulations, as well as ethical principles in research. Compliance with these standards will ensure the integrity of their operations and maintain public confidence.

Chapter 6: Countermeasures and Personal Protection Against OSINT

Open Source Intelligence (OSINT) is a powerful tool that can be used to gather information from publicly available sources. However, this easy access to data can also be used maliciously to gather personal information about individuals, companies, or organizations. In this chapter, we will look at countermeasures and personal protection strategies that everyone can put in place to guard against OSINT.

- **OSINT Personal Protection Policies**

To protect against OSINT and limit the collection of personal information, here are some practical strategies to consider:

- **Controlling Online Privacy Settings**

The first step to protecting against OSINT is to check and adjust privacy settings on online platforms. Social networks, business websites, and discussion forums usually have privacy settings that can be customized to limit the visibility of certain information. It is recommended that you restrict access to personal information to a restricted circle of trusted persons.

- **Social Media Management**

Social networks are often a major source of information for OSINT researchers. It's important to carefully review the information shared on social media and consider the potential implications of each post. Limiting the amount of personal information shared and avoiding disclosing sensitive details can help strengthen personal protection.

- **Use of Pseudonyms**

In some cases, the use of pseudonyms may be an option to protect against OSINT. Using a generic username rather than the real name on some websites or forums may reduce the possibility of being identified online.

- **Caution when Online Communication**

It is essential to exercise caution when communicating online with strangers. Avoid disclosing sensitive personal information to people you don't know personally. Be aware of the potential risks of social engineering, where attackers might try to gather information by pretending to be someone else.

- **Password Security**

Password security is crucial to protect online accounts from unauthorized access. Use strong, unique passwords for each account, and consider using a password manager to securely manage and store your credentials.

- **Monitoring Personal Information Online**

Regularly research your own name and personal information to see what information is available online. If sensitive information is found, consider contacting the appropriate sources to request deletion or updating of the information.

- **Social Engineering Awareness**

Social engineering awareness is essential to recognize attempts to manipulate or gather information by malicious actors. Educate yourself on common social engineering techniques and be cautious when responding to online inquiries.

- **Use of Information Deletion Tools**

There are online tools that allow you to remove personal information from public databases. By using these tools, you can reduce the amount of information available online.

- **Using a VPN**

Using a virtual private network (VPN) can add an extra layer of protection by masking your IP address and encrypting your internet connection. This can make it harder to collect information about your online activities.

- **OSINT Awareness**

In addition to putting in place personal protection measures, it is important to be aware of the existence of OSINT and its implications. By understanding how information can be collected from public sources, everyone can make informed decisions about what they share online and how they share it. Increased awareness of OSINT can help protect personal information and reduce the risk of data misuse.

- **Conclusion**

Personal protection against OSINT is essential at a time when personal information is increasingly accessible online. By understanding OSINT's risks and implementing protection strategies, everyone can help keep their personal information confidential. OSINT awareness is also crucial to making informed decisions about what to share online and how to share it. By taking a proactive approach and exercising caution, it is possible to guard against the potential risks of OSINT and effectively protect one's personal information.

Chapter 7: OSINT and the Dark Web: Exploring the Hidden Depths of the Internet

The Dark Web, this mysterious and obscure part of the Internet, is often associated with criminal activity, illegal markets, and underground networks. In this chapter, we will explore how OSINT can be used to securely access the dark web, gather information about illicit online activity, and understand the challenges and limitations associated with mining dark web data.

- **1. Understanding the Dark Web**

Before diving into OSINT's exploration of the Dark Web, it is essential to understand what the Dark Web really is and distinguish it from the Deep Web and the Web Surface. The Deep Web refers to all parts of the Internet that are not indexed by conventional search engines and require login credentials to access them, while the Surface Web represents the websites we use on a daily basis.

The Dark Web, on the other hand, is a part of the Deep Web that is accessible only through virtual private networks (VPNs) and the anonymous Tor browser. Tor is a decentralized network of computers that allows users to browse anonymously, masking their IP addresses and encrypting their communications. It is important to point out that although the Dark Web is home to illegal activities, it is not exclusively dedicated to it. It can also be used by people seeking to protect their privacy, journalists, whistleblowers, and others who need a safe and anonymous way to communicate.

- **2. Access and Browsing the Dark Web**

Access to the dark web requires the use of technologies that guarantee anonymity and confidentiality. We'll explore how to access the dark web safely, using tools like VPNs and the Tor browser. The VPN helps mask the user's real IP address by replacing it with the IP address of the VPN server, while the Tor browser uses onion routing to encrypt communications and hide where the connection is coming from.

We will also discuss best practices for browsing the dark web to avoid security risks and potential attacks. It is essential to remain vigilant and never download or execute suspicious files, as this may compromise the security of the device used to access the dark web.

- **3. Dark Web Resources for OSINT**

The Dark Web hosts a multitude of resources that can be used for OSINT. Forums, online marketplaces, chat rooms, anonymous blogs, and social networks are some examples of potential sources of information. In this section, we'll explore how investigators can quietly and ethically collect information on the Dark Web.

It is important to note that OSINT on the dark web presents specific challenges, as many sites require prior identification to access it. This means that investigators must be careful and abide by applicable laws when collecting information on the dark web.

- **4. Analysis of Criminal Activities**

One of the most common uses of OSINT on the dark web is the analysis of criminal activity. The Dark Web is home to a large number of illegal markets where everything from drugs and weapons can be found to stolen personal data and hacking kits.

Investigators can use OSINT to identify sellers and buyers involved in these illicit activities, track transactions of cryptocurrencies used for payments, and gather evidence for criminal investigations. However, it is important to note that OSINT on the dark web can be risky, as criminals are often very suspicious and take steps to protect their identity.

- **5. Limitations and Challenges of Dark Web OSINT**

It is essential to recognize the limitations and challenges associated with using OSINT on the dark web. First of all, the reliability of sources is often questioned, as information on the dark web can be manipulated, false or exaggerated. In addition, access to certain parts of the Dark Web may be restricted or require advanced technical skills.

Investigators must also consider security risks, as the dark web is a hostile environment where attacks can be launched against unsuspecting users. In addition, the use of OSINT on the dark web must be done in accordance with applicable laws and regulations, as some activities may be illegal in some jurisdictions.

- **6. OSINT Ethics on the Dark Web**

Ethics is a crucial aspect of OSINT on the Dark Web. Investigators should be aware of the risks associated with gathering information on illegal or potentially dangerous sites. It is essential to respect the privacy of individuals, not to contribute to illegal activities, and to comply with applicable laws and regulations.

OSINT on the Dark Web is a highly specialized skill that requires extensive training and understanding of ethical issues. OSINT professionals must act responsibly and respectfully when exploring the Dark Web.

Chapter 8: Going Further

In this final chapter, we will explore additional resources to deepen your knowledge of OSINT. Whether you are a beginner or an experienced professional, these sources will offer you opportunities to train, exchange with other enthusiasts, and stay at the forefront of this constantly evolving discipline.

- **Francophone OSINT forums**

Francophone forums dedicated to OSINT are spaces of exchange where intelligence or cybersecurity enthusiasts meet to discuss topics related to OSINT. These forums provide a platform to ask questions, share knowledge, and exchange tips and best practices. Popular Francophone forums include:

The "OSINT France" Forum: An active community of OSINT experts and enthusiasts who regularly share information on tools, techniques and news in the field.

The "Hackademics" forum: A discussion space where OSINT professionals and enthusiasts can exchange ideas, tutorials, and resources in French.

- **English-language OSINT forums**

In addition to the French-language forums, the English-language forums offer a wealth of information and discussion on OSINT. These forums are often attended by international experts in various OSINT-related fields. Popular English-language forums include:

The OSINT Curious Forum: A vibrant community of experts and enthusiasts who share their knowledge and experiences in OSINT.
The "Reddit OSINT" forum: A space on Reddit where users share links, news, and OSINT tips.

- **English-language books on OSINT**

For those who wish to deepen their knowledge of OSINT, there is a selection of books in English written by renowned experts. These books cover a variety of topics, ranging from information gathering techniques to methods of data analysis and exploitation. Some popular books include:

"Open Source Intelligence Techniques" by Michael Bazzell: A comprehensive guide to OSINT techniques with practical examples and tools recommended by the author.

"The OSINT Curious Project" by Justin Nordine: A collaborative book that brings together the knowledge and skills of a community of OSINT experts.

- **OSINT training**
  - *IHEDN War School*

The Institut des Hautes Études de Défense Nationale (IHEDN) is a French institution of higher education, whose mission is to train senior executives of the Nation in the fields of defense, security and strategic intelligence.

The IHEDN War School offers OSINT training modules as part of its programs on security, defense, and strategic intelligence. These courses are designed to meet the needs of professionals who wish to acquire advanced information gathering or intelligence skills.

OSINT training at IHEDN covers various topics, such as online search techniques, collection and analysis of information from public sources, verification of data authenticity, protection of privacy and personal data, and ethical use of OSINT in the context of intelligence and security.

The courses are taught by recognized experts in the field of OSINT and include real-life case studies for a better understanding of the practical issues. Participants have the opportunity to put their knowledge into practice through practical exercises and simulations.

- *EGE: School of Economic Warfare*

The EGE : École de Guerre Économique is a French institution specialized in training in economic intelligence. Founded in 1997, the EGE offers training for professionals, companies, and actors in the economic sphere to help them anticipate and manage risks related to competition and economic threats.

As part of its training in economic intelligence, the EGE also includes specific modules on OSINT. These modules aim to train participants in the use of open sources for the collection of relevant information on economic and financial topics.

OSINT training at EGE covers advanced research techniques, data analysis, online information monitoring, competitive intelligence, and understanding information security issues in the economic context.

Participants benefit from the expertise of professionals in business intelligence, cybersecurity, and information management. The courses also include case studies and practical exercises to enable participants to apply their skills in real-life situations.

- o Benefits of OSINT Training

The OSINT training offered by IHEDN War School and EGE has several advantages for participants:

Technical Skills Acquisition: Participants develop advanced skills in collecting and analyzing information from open sources, which enables them to collect relevant data and exploit it strategically.

Knowledge of Tools and Methods: The trainings introduce the most effective tools and methods for collecting information online, enabling participants to become knowledgeable users of OSINT resources.

Understanding of Security and Ethical Issues: The trainings raise participants' awareness of security and ethical issues related to OSINT, helping them to adopt a responsible approach in the use of the information collected.

Networking and Exchanges: Participants have the opportunity to meet other OSINT and business intelligence professionals, which promotes the exchange of good practices and opportunities for collaboration.

Practical Application: Courses include practical exercises and real-life case studies, allowing participants to practice their skills in real-world situations.

Conclusion: The impact of OSINT on our society

Online information gathering, commonly known as OSINT (Open Source Intelligence), has undergone significant evolution in recent decades and has gained increasing importance in our digital society. From national security and individual privacy to justice, cybersecurity and countering disinformation, OSINT influences various aspects of our daily lives.

In national security and intelligence, the collection of information from open sources plays a crucial role in monitoring potential threats, preventing terrorist activity, and responding to international crises. Governments and intelligence agencies rely on this practice to obtain information on foreign actors and analyze geopolitical strategies.

In the field of justice and law enforcement, OSINT is an invaluable tool for solving criminal investigations and combating cybercrime. Law enforcement uses this approach to track down criminals, gather digital evidence, and prepare strong legal cases. Lawyers and prosecutors also use the OSINT to obtain information about suspects and witnesses.

At the same time, OSINT plays a leading role in cybersecurity. IT security professionals use this approach to monitor hacker activity, identify vulnerabilities in systems, and detect ongoing cyberattacks. Collecting information online allows them to better understand the tactics and techniques used by cybercriminals, strengthening digital defenses.

However, the collection of information online also raises important ethical questions regarding the protection of privacy and personal data. The collection and use of information without the consent of individuals can compromise their privacy and security. It is therefore essential to strike a balance between the legitimate use of OSINT and the protection of individual rights.

In addition, OSINT plays a key role in the fight against disinformation. In a world where fake news and disinformation are spreading rapidly, OSINT makes it possible to verify sources, cross-reference information and rigorously analyze data. This approach helps to promote transparency and accuracy of information.

Constant technological change brings new challenges and opportunities to online information gathering. The emergence of artificial intelligence, machine learning and big data analysis opens up new perspectives for OSINT. However, these advances also raise questions about the automation and ethics of this approach.

To adapt to technological changes and new online threats, continuous training is essential for OSINT professionals. Techniques, tools, and information sources are evolving rapidly, and it's crucial to stay up-to-date with the latest trends and best practices in online information gathering and analysis.

In conclusion, collecting information online has a significant impact on our society. It offers invaluable opportunities for national security, justice, cybersecurity and the fight against disinformation. However, its use must be framed by ethical and privacy considerations. With a balanced and responsible approach, OSINT can be a powerful tool to improve safety, efficiency and transparency in our ever-changing society.

Éditions du Château – All rights reserved
August 2023

Printed in Great Britain
by Amazon